PCSSA - Pega Certified Senior System Architect Exam Practice Questions & Dumps

Exam Practice Questions For PCSSA Exam Prep LATEST VERSION

PRESENTED BY: Quantic Books

About Quantic Books:

Quantic Books is a publishing house based in Princeton, New Jersey, USA. , a platform that is accessible online as well as locally, which gives power to educational content, erudite collection, poetry & many other book genres. We make it easy for writers & authors to get their books designed, published, promoted, and sell professionally on worldwide scale with eBook + Print distribution. Quantic Books is now distributing books worldwide.

About Quantic Books:

Quantic Books is a publishing house based in Princeton, New Jersey, USA. , a platform that is accessible online as well as locally, which gives power to educational content, erudite collection, poetry & many other book genres. We make it easy for writers & authors to get their books designed, published, promoted, and sell professionally on worldwide scale with eBook + Print distribution. Quantic Books is now distributing books worldwide.

Note: Find answers of the questions at the last of the book.

QUESTION 1

A client's access group has two roles listeD. ? RoleA and RoleB (in that order).? RoleA has the "Open Instances of Data-Admin-Operator-ID" set to 0, and RoleB has it set to 5. Assuming there is no Access Deny guideline, will this client be able to open an operator instance on a production system and why? (Select One)

A. Yes, the higher of the two production levels wins
B. Yes, access roles are applied until a role grants access
C. No, if any role is set to 0, access is not granted
D. No, all access roles needs to grant access

QUESTION 2

Where do you organize the timeout in PRPC? (Select One)

A. In the web.xml file
B. In the prconfig.xml file
C. In the access group
D. In the Guideline-Admin-System-Settings

QUESTION 3

If an Access Role to Object and an Access Deny guideline are defined on the same class, which guideline takes precedence with respect to security? (Select One)

A. Access Role to Object
B. Access Deny
C. PRPC prevents them from both being applied to the same class
D. None – they are both applied

QUESTION 4

A client has an access role that lets them Level 5 access to modify instances of the MyCo-Work-PolicyApp-Endorse class. Which guideline kind must you use to disallow access to instances of the MyCo-Work-PolicyApp-Endorse class? (Select One)

A. Access Settings
B. Access Role to Object
C. Access Deny
D. Access Privilege

QUESTION 5

(Accurate or Inaccurate) Even if you use a centralized directory (LDAP) and/or individuality management system for verification, you need to store Operator IDs in PRPC. (Select One)

A. Accurate. Every requestor in PRPC needs an associated Operator ID
B. Accurate. You need the Operator ID to bind to the LDAP directory
C. Inaccurate. You use the LDAP Client ID instead of the Operator ID
D. Inaccurate. This is only needed if you're reporting off of PRPC's database

QUESTION 6

There are two session-related timeouts that are configurable in PRPC, the verification timeout and the requestor timeout. Which report is accurate? (Select One)

A. Verification timeout must be set to happen first
B. Requestor timeout must be set to happen first
C. Both timeouts must be set to the same value
D. With passivation enabled, the verification timeout must be set to 0

QUESTION 7

Access groups cannot be referenced from which one of the next objects? (Select One)

A. Operator ID
B. WorkGroup
C. Organization
D. Division

QUESTION 8

Which one guideline kind cannot be associated with a privilege? (Select One)

A. Correspondence
B. ListView
C. Decision Table
D. Flow

QUESTION 9

A client has the next class access mappings: ? MyCo-App-Work
Modify Guidelines = 3 ? MyCo-App-Work-CaseCreate Modify
Guidelines = 5 ? MyCo-App-Work- CaseDelete Modify Guidelines =
0 Which three reports below are correct? (Select Three)

A. The client can modify guidelines in the MyCo-App-Work-
Research class on a Development system
B. The client can modify guidelines in the MyCo-App-Work-
CaseDelete class in an Experimental system
C. The client can modify guidelines in the MyCo-App-Work-
CaseCreate class in a Test system
D. The client can modify guidelines in the MyCo-App-Work-
CaseCreate class in Production

QUESTION 10

Given the diagram below, what kind of guideline is canPerform?
(Select One)

A. Access Privilege
B. Access Settings
C. Access When
D. Access Deny

QUESTION 11

Can the out-of-the-box (OOTB) PRPC Access Roles be modified?
(Select One)

A. No, all of these roles are in locked GuidelineSets

B. Yes, out-of-the-box roles are starter roles that are supposed to be customized

C. No, out-of-the-box roles must be overridden in application GuidelineSets

D. Yes, the Role Editor lets you to modify all roles

QUESTION 12

An activity (MyCo-Div1-.SaveQuote) is associated with the next privileges: ? mayQuote? maySaveA client has the maySave privilege but not the mayQuote privilege. Can the client run the activity?
(Select One)

A. No, the client needs to have all of the privileges listed on an activity to execute the activity

B. Yes, all shared guidelines can be executed by applications across the enterprise

C. Yes, if the client has any of the privileges listed on an activity, they may execute the activity

D. Yes, privileges on an activity only control design-time restrictions

QUESTION 13

How would you decide whether a requestor holds a specific privilege? (Select One)

A. Interrogate the Declare_PrivilegeName page on the clipboard
B. Make use of the PublicAPI. - tools.GetPrivilege(Requestor).Rolename method
C. Make use of the function: - @ (Pega-GUIDELINES:Default).HavePrivilege("tools", privname, privAppliesTo, pagename)
D. Use a section of Java and utilize the out-of-the-box (OOTB) ListRequestorPrivilege(Role r) method

QUESTION 14

Using the Access Role editor, you are able to___(Select Three)

A. get a tabular overview of all Access of Role to Object guidelines that make up an Access Role
B. create new privilege guidelines
C. view Operators mapped to selected Role
D. copy permissions to another role
E. create a new role
F. view Access Deny guidelines to a class

QUESTION 15

Which report is inaccurate about Guideline-HTML-Property instances? (Select One)

A. Guideline-HTML-Property instances can be circumstanced
B. Guideline-HTML-Property instances belong to a GuidelineSet version
C. Guideline-HTML-Property instances can accept parameters as input
D. Guideline-HTML-Property instances have an Applies To class

QUESTION 16

In which order does validation happen on a standard flow action? (Select One)

A. Client-Side Validation, Post Processing Activity, Validate Guideline on Flow Action
B. Client Side Validation, Validate Guideline on Flow Action, Post Processing Activity
C. Validate Guideline on Flow Action, Client-Side Validation, Post Processing Activity
D. You can change the order per screen

QUESTION 17

Which two of the next tools are primarily designed to help debug and develop the client interface layout for an application? (Select Two)

A. Guidelines Inspector
B. Tracer
C. Style Viewer
D. Pre Flight
E. Profiler

QUESTION 18

Which two reports are accurate about screen flows? (Select Two)

A. Define a single harness for the entire screen flow
B. Each step in the screen flow can be routed to different worklist or workbasket
C. Defer committing changes until the end of the screen flow, if organized to do so in the start shape with "Save Later" set to accurate
D. Each task in a screen flow lets for you to add more than one flow action

QUESTION 19

Which one report best explains how you can control navigation within a screen flow? (Select One)

A. Each step in the screen flow lets you to decide if you can jump to this step or if you can only jump back after it has been completed
B. Screen flows only support task shapes thus always have a pre-defined number of steps to complete
C. The harness defines if you are able to jump forward to future steps in a screen flow
D. Screen flows always force the end client to walk through the flow in sequential order without the ability to jump from one screen to another

QUESTION 20

Which client side events are supported within PRPC? (Select Three)

A. OnChange
B. OnMouseout
C. OnClick
D. OnBlur
E. OnFocus

QUESTION 21

According to Pega's best practice what is the referred way to execute a solution in this instance. You have a list of purchase orders on the screen, each with a price. As you change the price the Grand Total must automatically be updated. (Select One)

A. Put an OnChange client event on each of the price inputs and have it use the refresh section event to call an activity to calculate the Grand Total
B. Build a Declarative expression to calculate the Grand Total and use the CalculatedValue HTML-Property on the Grand Total property when displaying it
C. Build a Declarative expression to calculate the Grand Total and refresh the section when inputs change
D. Use OnChange client events on the input elements and have them alter the value in the Grand Total property

QUESTION 22

Which report is accurate about the initial harness that displays for a work object? (Select One)

A. The initial harness is defined in the pyDefault model
B. The initial harness is defined on every flow
C. The initial harness is only defined for flows that create new work objects and is required
D. The initial harness can be skipped and this is configurable from the flow guideline

QUESTION 23

Which of the next are inaccurate? (Select Three)

A. Repeating list displays are only for page lists
B. You can display lists as row or column lists (Top to Bottom or Left to Right)
C. You can only display a list as a row repeating list display (List goes from top to bottom)
D. There is no support for tabs when displaying repeating lists
E. A section guideline can be used to specify how items of the repeating list are displayed

QUESTION 24

Which four of the next are provided as out-of-the-box (OOTB) widgets when creating client interface guidelines? (Select Four)

A. List-to-List
B. Sliders
C. Dynamic Select
D. Toolbar
E. Auto Complete
F. List View

QUESTION 25

Which layouts are provided out-of-the-box (OOTB) when building forms? (Select Two)

A. Carousel Layout
B. Accordion Layout
C. Tabbed Layout
D. Concertina Layouts

QUESTION 26

Which one report describes the best practice for branding an application to meet a company's style requirements? (Select One)

A. Use the Application Skin wizard and then use inline styles on the client interface guidelines
B. Use the Application Skin wizard and then modify the generated skins when needed, try to limit inline styles
C. Only use the style viewer and make changes to the out-of-the-box CSS files and your own Guideline Sets
D. Use inline styles to change displays to meet corporate standards

QUESTION 27

Which are best practices when designing client interface guidelines so they can be re-used? (Select Two)

A. By building all displays within cells of layouts it will allow you the granularity needed to re-use the guideline

B. By building section guidelines or HTML-Property guidelines with parameters it will allow you to re-use these display guidelines more frequently within an application

C. By grouping related data into section guidelines, you can re-use these sections throughout the application and control if they must be updateable or read-only in the parent section

D. The best practice for re-using client interface guidelines is to assure it is in the right part of the class structure

QUESTION 28

Where do you organize the label that displays in the drop down at a task (i.e. the list of available actions)? (Select One)

A. It is set within the Task shape on the flow

B. It is set by the short description from the flow action guideline

C. It is set by the usage on the history tab on the flow action guideline

D. It is set by a parameter in the pre-activity on the flow action

QUESTION 29

Which features lets the worklist to display additional data from the work object? (Select Two)

A. The JOIN feature on List Views now lets you join the task table to the work object table to add exposed columns to the worklist display
B. The JOIN feature on List Views now lets you join the task table to the work object table to retrieve any element from the work object
C. The Smart Info hover over lets you display a Section guideline to show additional work object information
D. Alter the get Content activity to write custom code to look through items on worklist to perform additional lookups on the work table

QUESTION 30

When working with Client Interface guidelines such as Sections, it is possible to save them in the "work" or "data" portions of the class structure hierarchy. Is the next report accurate or inaccurate? Saving Section guidelines in the "data" portion of the hierarchy is usually better because the guidelines can then be reused wherever its associated data is used, without having to worry about correct property referencing.

A. Accurate
B. Inaccurate

QUESTION 31

Which tools gives you the broadest picture of your system's overall health? (Select Two)

A. PAL
B. Profiler
C. System Management Application (SMA)
D. DBTrace
E. Autonomic Event Services (AES)

QUESTION 32

Which two actions help to optimize your database or promote effective SQL reports? (Select Two)

A. Partition the database
B. Avoid arithmetic operations or functions in the SELECT clause
C. Write queries that operate on large results sets but only display small amounts of data
D. Create and use indexes effectively
E. Avoid using Where clauses

QUESTION 33

What are three performance impacts of having an extremely large work object? (Select Three)

A. Slower persistence to database as the BLOB needs to be compressed
B. Garbage collection impacts when object is released
C. Large clipboard page footprint
D. Large work objects waste space in the instance cache
E. Large work objects are stored as XML files on the file system and will lead to "out of disk" errors if they are not purged frequently

QUESTION 34

The PAL indicators that refer to the "stream" are measuring what? (Select One)

A. The HTML data going to the browser
B. Any processing of requests and responses via Services
C. Reading and writing data in the database
D. Database operations pertaining to the BLOB

QUESTION 35

What is the Byte Governor alert (PEGA0004) and how does it work? (Select Two)

A. It is a critical alert that can take the form of an alert or an error
B. It is triggered when the total number of bytes sent to the browser in an interaction exceeds a byte count threshold
C. It is triggered when the total number of bytes read from all queries in an interaction exceeds a byte count threshold
D. It is triggered when the total number of bytes saved to the database in an interaction exceeds a byte count threshold

QUESTION 36

Where do you customize the thresholds for alerts? (Select One)

A. PRLOGGING.XML
B. Guideline-Admin-System-Settings
C. PRCONFIG.XML
D. You cannot customize the thresholds; the defaults are fine and do not need to be adjusted

QUESTION 37

Which tool is best to use if you want to compare PRPC Errors with Alerts, as well as the JVM Garbage Collection Log? (Select One)

A. PLA – PegaGUIDELINES Log Analyzer
B. AES – Autonomic Event Services
C. SMA – System Management Application
D. Excel

QUESTION 38

Your application just went into production and the clients are complaining that response times are terrible. Your best initial action must be? (Select Two)

A. Use the PLA – PegaGUIDELINES Log Analyzer to analyze ALERTS, System Logs, and the GC (Garbage Collection)
B. Run PAL on every screen in the application
C. Run Pre-Flight
D. Check the Pega Alert logs

QUESTION 39

Which one of the next are accurate about DB Trace and Application Profiler? (Select Two)

A. They are essentially the same thing, it's a personal preference as to which to use
B. You can see Activity guideline executions only in the Application Profiler
C. To see where database actions are taking place, the Application Profiler provides more detail than DBTrace
D. The Application Profiler is the better tool to see step-by-step where the elapsed and CPU time is being spent

QUESTION 40

Why is allowing instances to be stored in a default table (pr_other) a poor design practice? (Select Two)

A. The default table does not contain adequate indexes and columns for performance
B. The default table does not have adequate exposed columns
C. The default table names are too generic
D. The default table is too small to hold all of your data
E. Because the Preflight tool will flag it as bad practice

QUESTION 41

Which three of the next measurements are used by the alerts reported to the PRPC Alert log? (Select Three)

A. The overall time elapsed from when a client triggers Client Side JavaScript
B. The time spent executing Declarative expressions
C. The time for a response from a web service called using the Connect-SOAP method
D. The time for a database query to execute and return results to PRPC
E. The size of the HTML stream returned to the client/browser

QUESTION 42

Which one of the next reports is accurate? (Select One)

A. The overall size of a PRPC work object impacts the time it takes to compress and store the object in the database
B. During List View execution, PRPC will only retrieve/expand the BLOB if the properties retrieved are not exposed
C. During List View execution, PRPC will only retrieve/expand the BLOB if the properties used in the generated Where clause are not exposed
D. PRPC only retrieves/expands the BLOB via the use of the Obj-Open and Obj-Open-By-Handle methods
E. By default the PRPC BLOB is stored in an encrypted format in the database

QUESTION 43

Which of the next reports are accurate about PRPC and garbage collection? (Select Two)
A. Effective clipboard management is one of the best ways for an architect to reduce an applications memory footprint and time spent in performing garbage collection
B. When available, additional JVM heap space may or may not improve the time spent in garbage collection
C. As PRPC architects it is important to set properties to null so that they can be discarded as part of garbage collection
D. As long as reporting is done by a 3rd party tool garbage collection will have minimal impact on the performance of a PRPC application

QUESTION 44

Given the next situation:
A BPM application was deployed into production nine months ago and was performing well initially. Now, clients complain of slow response times on certain screen interactions irrespective of the time of day. Which one of the next reports is most likely to be accurate as to the root cause of this issue? (Select One)

A. Over time more rows have been added to work, history, task and operator tables and inefficient queries against those tables are taking longer than they did 9 months earlier
B. A memory leak in the configuration has led to more and more garbage collection over the past nine months
C. If the PRPC application server has not be restarted recently it is likely the case that the PRPC caches have filled up and are not being utilized well
D. As new guidelines have been added to the PRPC guideline base, the database containing the guidelines needs to be properly indexed and tuned so that frequent access to the guidelines is made as efficient as possible

QUESTION 45

Which two reports are inaccurate about the Log-Message method? (Select Two)

A. You can force a stack trace
B. You can specify the filename where you want to write the message
C. It lets you to avoid using Java steps to write to the Page GUIDELINES log
D. You can add a message that will show up in Tracer
E. It always uses the Debug log level

QUESTION 46

Which one of the next is not a refactoring tool provided by PRPC?
(Select One)

A. Renaming a class and propagating the name change through the
hierarchy and guideline references
B. Converting a Map-Value into a Decision Table
C. Search and replace of a string in all guidelines
D. Merging one GuidelineSet into another

QUESTION 47

Which feature is available when using Tracer? (Select One)

A. You can set a breakpoint for a specific step within an activity
B. Open an named clipboard page to display current data
C. Select which requestor session you wish to trace, using the SMA
tool
D. Re-run a specific set of steps with updated data

QUESTION 48

How can you debug an agent using Tracer? (Select One)

A. There is a way to select the agent and force its execution
B. You can trace a given requestor by delaying an agent in SMA
C. You can set a break point in the activity that the agent runs to
have Tracer pick it up
D. You can set a log-message step in the activity the agent runs to
have Tracer find the activity

QUESTION 49

Which two reports are accurate about configuring log files in PRPC? (Select Two)

A. You cannot organize within an Activity guideline to which log file you want to write errors

B. You are able to organize within SMA which guidelines write to which log files

C. You can update prlogging.xml file to change the default PegaGUIDELINES log file names

D. You can update the prlogging.xml file to change the log file names, roll over settings and even add new log files for specific guideline kind and class within PRPC

QUESTION 50

Which of the next caches maintains references to the java class generated when a Flow guideline is executed against a work object for the first time? (Select One)

A. Guidelines Assembly cache

B. Guideline cache

C. Lookup List cache

D. Personal cache

QUESTION 51

All of the next are ways in which you can access system logs except: (Select Two)

A. From the Developer menu selecting; Tools > Log Files

B. Clicking the Save icon from the Tracer tool

C. From the System Management Application menu selecting ; Logging and Tracing > Log Files

D. Remote logging using log4j

E. Through the prdbutil interface

QUESTION 52

You are unit testing your flow and have meticulously clicked "Add Reading" at every transition. The result is below. Is this a fair reflection of the likely performance of your flow? (Select One)

A. Yes, there's nothing wrong with it
B. No, it shows clear performance issues
C. No, you must run it again; these results have been skewed by guidelines assembly

QUESTION 53

Which one of the next reports about logging is inaccurate? (Select One)

A. All log messages are written to either the Alert log or the Pega log
B. Log severity level can be organized for guidelines, guideline kinds, activities, classes and packages
C. The alert threshold settings are organized in prlogging.xml
D. The severity levels of logging are: fatal, error, alert, warn, info, and debug
E. Daily rolling logs are organized in prlogging.xml

QUESTION 54

Which two of the next reports are accurate about Summary Views?
(Select Two)

A. Summary View reports provide a multi-level report display with drill-down capabilities
B. The 'drill down' capability provides only the ability to invoke another Summary View guideline
C. Because of the aggregate first-level display, Summary Views allow you to report on very large report sets of 10,000 rows or more
D. Summary View guidelines generate HTML and JSP for display that can be further customized

QUESTION 55

Which three out-of-the-box (OOTB) features do List Views provide?
(Select Three)

A. Pagination
B. Defining thresholds
C. Single or multi-selection
D. Trend Reporting
E. Class Joins

QUESTION 56

Which three reports are accurate about List View reports? (Select Three)

A. A List View report can be displayed in a flow action
B. Both developers and managers can create and update List View guidelines
C. In an activity, a List View guideline can be executed to provide searching and sorting, with no display, as an efficient alternative to the Obj-List method
D. List View reports can only run queries against PRPC task and work object tables

QUESTION 57

Pick the one most appropriate report about PRPC reporting. (Select One)

A. PRPC is an excellent reporting solution and is referred for reporting instead of purchasing expensive Business Intelligence reporting software
B. You can always get the reporting data you need by exposing properties as database columns
C. If the reporting data is stored in sources other than PRPC, you need to create connectors to retrieve the data from the source system
D. PRPC reporting is highly optimized; the impact of running large reports in a production system is negligible
E. PRPC includes powerful Business Activity Monitoring reports that provide business managers with real-time and historical information to measure and manage business process performance

QUESTION 58

Which three reports are accurate about the out-of-the-box (OOTB) PRPC reports? (Select Three)

A. A database view can simplify reporting, especially with properties from two or more classes that are in separate class groups
B. Reports in the Monitor Processes category support day-to-day monitoring of the backlogs of work that has arrived but is incomplete
C. Reports in the Analyze Performance group analyze which flow actions were selected how often, by task, and the timeliness of the selection
D. Analyze Performance and Analyze Quality reports cover only unresolved work objects
E. Monitor Tasks and Monitor Processes reports cover resolved work objects only
F. The Final Conflicts report lets developers to identify guidelines in the current application GuidelineSet version that conflict with previous GuidelineSet versions

QUESTION 59

Which two of the next reports are accurate about exposing BLOB data? (Select Two)

A. Declare Expression or Declare Trigger guidelines can be used to copy a single embedded property to a top-level property, and this top-level property can be exposed
B. Declare Index guidelines can be used to expose many, or all, of the items in an embedded list or group
C. Ask your DBA to create a database-level index, because this is a good mechanism to expose embedded properties
D. Exposing a new property with the Modify Database Schema wizard will automatically populate all rows of the respective database column – both for new rows and existing ones

QUESTION 60

Which two reports are accurate about SmartInfo displays? (Select Two)

A. May utilize input fields
B. SmartInfo can display as a popup window or embedded
C. The SmartInfo feature is part of Client-Side processing and handled completely by the browser
D. The SmartInfo display can contain images

QUESTION 61

Which three reports are accurate about Summary View and List View reports? (Select Three)

A. Summary View reports allow you to drill down to another Summary View report
B. Summary View reports allow you to drill down to a detailed view
C. Both summary views and list views provide client side and server side filtering capabilities in addition to the database "where" clause
D. List views allow you to pass in parameter values to be used as selection criteria
E. Parameters can be used to override selection criteria that are hard-coded in a summary view

QUESTION 62

Which two reports are accurate about the Report Wizard? (Select Two)

A. The Report Wizard can only be used to create reports on work
B. Using the wizard will ensure best possible performance of your report
C. You can use the Report Wizard to delegate created reports to an access group
D. You need a special privilege to run the Report Wizard

QUESTION 63

Which two reports are accurate about reports? (Select Two)

A. List View and Summary View guidelines allow you to present the results in segments, known as pages
B. The criteria specified in Filter By become part of the SQL WHERE clause
C. Paging improves response time and reduces the size of the clipboard
D. The report display generated by a list view can be embedded in a section

QUESTION 64

Which two reports are accurate about the getContent activity? (Select Two)

A. The getContent activity must not be replaced as it provides highly optimized retrieval of reporting data
B. You can customize the getContent activity by creating a copy of the same name in your application GuidelineSet
C. Creating a custom getContent-like activity that is specified as the report source lets you to fetch data from sources other than databases
D. Data can be fetched from an external database table so long as the key of the table is mapped to the pxInsHandle property

QUESTION 65

Which two reports are accurate about reports? (Select Two)

A. Summary views allow you to drill down into another Summary View, List View, or a Detailed View

B. Both List View and Summary View guidelines can use an override sort function

C. Both List View and Summary View guidelines can use class joins to reference properties from multiple classes

D. Only List View guidelines may use parameter

QUESTION 66

Which of the next is accurate? (Select One)

A. You can test the persistence connectivity for a class on the Class guideline form, on the associated Data-Admin-DB-Table record, as well as on the Class Structure Viewer

B. All four foundation classes (Guideline-Obj-Class, Data-Admin-DB-Table, Data-Admin-DB-Name, Data-Admin-DB-ClassGroup) needs to be stored in pr4_guideline table

C. One can use Obj- methods to the PRPC database to read/write data to the work-object tables without impact on data integrity

D. Process commander searches the Data-Admin-DB-Table using the pattern and direct inheritance mechanism to find the table that stores the instances of a given class

QUESTION 67

Which one action must you not take when designing for guideline delegation? (Select One)

A. Select guideline names and property names that are meaningful in the business context
B. Identify which guidelines are useful to delegate to managers for maintenance
C. Ensure that the GuidelineSet(s) that contain the delegated guidelines are part of the Application Guideline, not the Production GuidelineSet list
D. After initial testing, copy the guidelines into a GuidelineSet containing only the delegated guidelines so that later changes can be segregated from the rest of the application
E. Make sure the delegated GuidelineSet is locked

QUESTION 68

Which groups of guideline kinds use Functions Alias guidelines on their guideline forms? (Select One)

A. Decision trees, Map values and Decision tables
B. Declare expressions, activities and Guideline-Access-When
C. Decision trees, Map values, and Guideline-Declare-Constraint
D. Decision trees, When guidelines, and Declare expressions

QUESTION 69

Which two of the next are Declarative guidelines? (Select Two)

A. Guideline-Declare-DecisionTree
B. Guideline-Declare-DecisionTable
C. Guideline-Obj-MapValue
D. Guideline-Declare-Expression
E. Guideline-Declare-OnChange

QUESTION 70

Which one of the next guidelines can use backward chaining as a method of propagation? (Select One)

A. Guideline-Declare-Expression

B. Guideline-Declare-OnChange

C. Guideline-Declare-Constraints

D. Guideline-Declare-Trigger

E. Guideline-Declare-CaseMatch

QUESTION 71

During the execution of a Guideline-Declare-OnChange will declarative expressions execute? (Select One)

Yes
No

QUESTION 72

Which one of the next guidelines lets you to copy the previous value
of one property to another property if you want to audit property
level changes? (Select One)

A. Guideline-Declare-OnChange
B. Guideline-Declare-Trigger
C. Guideline-Declare-Expression
D. Guideline-Declare-DecisionTree
E. Guideline-Obj-MapValue

QUESTION 73

Select three times when a Thread level Declarative page is removed
from memory? (Select Three)

A. When the client does not refer to it for a duration more than the
   timeout setting
B. When the client logs out
C. When the client session expires
D. When the application server is brought down
E. When the SMA is used to "refresh" a declarative page

QUESTION 74

As part of a BRE execution, is it possible to execute unordered guidelines dynamically if given a set of conditions that statE. execute all Decision guidelines when State is Ohio, and audit as to which guidelines get executed? (Select One)

A. No PRPC has no (out-of-the-box (OOTB) facilities to support this and we will have to build something custom to support this
B. Yes, you can do this using a List View in conjunction with a Guideline-Declare-Collection
C. Yes, you can do this using a Summary View in conjunction with Guideline-Declare-Collection
D. Yes, you can do this using a Guideline-Declare-Expression in conjunction with a Guideline-Declare-CaseMatch
E. Yes you can do this using a Guideline-Declare-Trigger in conjunction with Guideline-Obj-MapValue

QUESTION 75

If you created a Guideline-Declare-Expression guideline on a target property A first, will PRPC let you to use property A in the left hand side of a Property-Set in a new activity? (Select One)

A. Yes
B. No

QUESTION 76

The calculation kinds (e.g. Sum Of, Value Of, etc) available in a Declare Expressions guideline are_____? (Select One)

A. Dependent on the "applies to" class of the guideline
B. Dependent on if the expression is context-free or context sensitive
C. Dependent on the kind of the input properties
D. Dependent on the kind of the target property

QUESTION 77

Which of the next is a difference between a Declarative Page defined as Node level versus Thread level? (Select One)

A. Node level pages are read-only and thread level are not
B. Thread level pages can use a when to decide when the page needs to refresh, node level cannot
C. Only Node level pages needs to be named Declare_Node_<PageName>
D. Node level pages are loaded when PRPC starts up and thread level pages are loaded when the client logs in

QUESTION 78

Guideline-Declare-OnChange guidelines are different from
Guideline-Declare-Expressions in that? (Select One)

A. OnChange guidelines can directly execute an activity in a
   background process rather than set a single property
B. Expressions allow configuring of the execution context to any, top
   level, or only specific pages
C. OnChange guidelines fire when designated properties change on
   the clipboard as opposed to expressions which require a
   database commit
D. OnChange guidelines ONLY use backward chaining to track
   changes whereas expressions can use either forward or
   backward chaining

QUESTION 79

Which of the next is accurate? (Select One)

A. Decision Tables can call only Decision Trees without having to
   use a utility function
B. Decision Trees can only call other Decision Trees without having
   to use a utility function
C. Decision Trees can call other Decision Trees, Decision Table or
   Map Values without having to use a utility function
D. Decision Tables can call other Decision Tables, Decision Trees
   or Map Values without having to use a utility function

QUESTION 80

(Accurate or Inaccurate) Decision tables can associate a privilege with the ability to edit each individual cell.

A. Accurate
B. Inaccurate

QUESTION 81

A Guideline-Declare-Page named Declare_RichieTest is of page scope Thread. It has a Refresh period of five minutes and no timeout. There is also a "Page is fresh when" guideline "CodIsInStock" based on a Accurate/Inaccurate property CodIsInStock Consider this sequence of events: – Declare_RichieTest is first accessed and loaded at 14:34– CodStock is set to inaccurate at 14:38– Declare_RichieTest is next accessed at 14:45When is the Declare_RichieTest page loaded again? (Select One)

A. 14:45
B. 14:39
C. 14:38
D. Never, once loaded the page is never reloaded

QUESTION 82

Which of the next is inaccurate about Declarative Pages? (Select One)

A. Load Activity kind needs to be set to "LoadDeclarativePage"
B. Only Node level declare pages prompt you to organize an Access Group. If left blank, Requestor Access Group is used
C. Refresh conditions can be organized on guideline form
D. Only Thread pages may utilize the "Refresh Page When" option to refresh the page
E. Cannot be directly saved to database

QUESTION 83

Which three reports are accurate about primary and step pages within activities? (Select Three)

A. A primary page acts as the context for the entire activity
B. A step in an activity where the Step Page column is blank indicates that the step page is the primary page
C. When iterating through embedded pages, each instance of the embedded page becomes the step page for that step
D. When an activity calls another guideline, the primary page of the calling activity becomes the primary page of the called guideline
E. The primary keyword always refers to a top-level page

QUESTION 84

What are the 6 R's? (Select Six)

A. Repeat
B. Reply
C. Reserve
D. Report
E. Re-examine
F. Receive
G. Return
H. Resolve
I. Respond
J. ROI
K. Route
L. Research

QUESTION 85

When is it appropriate to use a sub-flow shape instead of a spin-off flow shape? (Select One)

A. When you wish to run calculations in a separate thread from the current process
B. When you wish to perform work on a different work object
C. When you want to transfer control to another flow guideline
D. When you wish to route work to a different department while continuing down the current process path

QUESTION 86

Which two of the next reports are accurate about the Split-For-Each and Split-Join shapes? (Select Two)

A. Both shapes allow you to continue processing when ANY or ALL of the sub processes complete

B. Split-Join lets you to execute different sub-flows whereas Split-For-Each calls the same process on different pages

C. Split-For-Each lets you to execute different sub-flows whereas Split-Join calls the same process on different pages.

D. Both shapes create separate Threads for sub-processes they create

E. Split-For-Each can only be used when iterating over a list of work objects

QUESTION 87

Which one of the next reports is accurate about the execution of PRPC's Spin-Off flow behavior? (Select One)

A. Spin-Off flows are executed in the current requestor in a serial manner; however they do provide business parallelism by allowing multiple clients to have tasks on the same work object

B. Spin-Off flows achieve greater throughput by allowing tasks to be worked on by multiple clients at the same time by obtaining a separate lock for each sub- process

C. Spin-Off flows create separate Threads which allow for faster processing of tasks and calculations

D. Spin-Off flows create separate requestors so that work can be assigned to different clients

QUESTION 88

Which two of the next reports are accurate about the use of Draft Flows? (Select Two)

A. Draft flows allow clients to directly capture processes without requiring referenced guidelines to be completed
B. Draft flows can be executed to demonstrate the process
C. Draft flows can only be executed if a previous, non-draft-mode version exists
D. Once a flow is checked in it cannot be marked as a draft flow. You can't change the status of a checked in guideline, can you?
E. Draft flows can only be executed if the flow actions they reference have been created

QUESTION 89

Which one of the next reports are accurate about passing page references to activities? (Select One)

A. Both page name parameters and prompt pages provide a way to pass a page reference to an activity so page names don't need to be hardcoded
B. Page name parameters can only be used to pass top-level pages
C. Page names parameters create aliases for pages that can be used by any guideline that is executed after an activity
D. Passing pages by reference requires java code

QUESTION 90

Which two of the next reports are accurate? (Select Two)

A. Task and work object SLAs allow for separate service levels to be defined on individual tasks and overall work resolution
B. Work object SLAs are normally specified in a model but can be modified during subsequent processing
C. Work object SLAs can only be set during work object creation
D. Task SLAs default to the work object SLA if not specified
E. Work object SLAs are defined on the start shape of a flow and are overwritten by SLAs on individual tasks

QUESTION 91

Which one of the next is accurate about the concepts of push and pull routing as executed in PRPC? (Select One)

A. Assigning work to a worklist is an instance of push routing and using get next work to grab work from a workbasket is an instance of pull routing

B. Assigning work to a worklist is an instance of pull routing and using get next work to grab work from a workbasket is an instance of push routing

C. Using a load balancing algorithm to assign work to individual operators is an instance of pull routing

D. A single application must only use one kind of routing, push or pull

QUESTION 92

Out of the Box Get Next Work functionality is NOT useful in solving which one of the next business problems? (Select One)

A. The "cherry-picking" of easy work selected first from workbaskets causing some work to not be done in a timely manner
B. Retrieving work based on highest urgency
C. Evenly distributing work to all members of a team
D. Retrieving work from one or more workbaskets or worklist

ANSWERS

1. Correct Answer: B
2. Correct Answer: C
3. Correct Answer: B
4. Correct Answer: C
5. Correct Answer: A
6. Correct Answer: A
7. Correct Answer: B
8. Correct Answer: C
9. Correct Answer: ACD
10. Correct Answer: C
11. Correct Answer: A
12. Correct Answer: C
13. Correct Answer: C
14. Correct Answer: ADE
15. Correct Answer: D
16. Correct Answer: B
17. Correct Answer: AC
18. Correct Answer: AC
19. Correct Answer: A
20. Correct Answer: ACD
21. Correct Answer: B
22. Correct Answer: D
23. Correct Answer: ACD
24. Correct Answer: ACEF
25. Correct Answer: BC
26. Correct Answer: B
27. Correct Answer: BC
28. Correct Answer: B
29. Correct Answer: AC
30. Correct Answer: A
31. Correct Answer: CE
32. Correct Answer: AD
33. Correct Answer: ABC
34. Correct Answer: D
35. Correct Answer: AC
36. Correct Answer: C
37. Correct Answer: A
38. Correct Answer: AD
39. Correct Answer: CD
40. Correct Answer: AB
41. Correct Answer: CDE
42. Correct Answer: A

43. Correct Answer: AB
44. Correct Answer: A
45. Correct Answer: BE
46. Correct Answer: B
47. Correct Answer: C
48. Correct Answer: B
49. Correct Answer: AD
50. Correct Answer: A
51. Correct Answer: BE
52. Correct Answer: C
53. Correct Answer: C
54. Correct Answer: AC
55. Correct Answer: ACE
56. Correct Answer: ABC
57. Correct Answer: E
58. Correct Answer: ABC
59. Correct Answer: AB
60. Correct Answer: BD
61. Correct Answer: ABD
62. Correct Answer: CD
63. Correct Answer: CD
64. Correct Answer: CD
65. Correct Answer: AC
66. Correct Answer: C
67. Correct Answer: C
68. Correct Answer: D
69. Correct Answer: DE
70. Correct Answer: A
71. Correct Answer: B
72. Correct Answer: B
73. Correct Answer: BCD
74. Correct Answer: B
75. Correct Answer: B
76. Correct Answer: D
77. Correct Answer: B
78. Correct Answer: B
79. Correct Answer: C
80. Correct Answer: B
81. Correct Answer: A
82. Correct Answer: B
83. Correct Answer: ABC
84. Correct Answer: DFHIKL
85. Correct Answer: C
86. Correct Answer: AB

87. Correct Answer: A
88. Correct Answer: AB
89. Correct Answer: A
90. Correct Answer: AB
91. Correct Answer: A
92. Correct Answer: C

Printed in Great Britain
by Amazon